D'Nealian Handwriting Readiness

for Preschoolers

Book 1

Donald N. Thurber

Scott, Foresman and Company

Glenview, Illinois   *London*

Copyright © 1987 Scott, Foresman and Company.
All Rights Reserved.
Printed in the United States of America.

ISBN 0-673-18855-8

1819-EBI-9998

D'Nealian® Handwriting Readiness
for Preschoolers
Book 2
A second-level readiness practice book that reviews the finger-tracing technique and goes one step further to writing with a crayon.
By Donald N. Thurber, 32 pages, paperback
ISBN 0-673-18856-6

D'Nealian® Home/School Activities
Manuscript Practice for Grades 1–3
Clear directions for forming each lower- and upper-case letter of the alphabet, plus numbers, with space provided for practice. Maintains and reinforces manuscript writing skills.
By Donald N. Thurber, 64 pages, paperback
ISBN 0-673-18535-4

D'Nealian® Home/School Activities
Cursive Practice for Grades 4–6
More than 125 ready-to-use activities, ranging from simple cursive practice to imaginative assignments that develop thinking and writing skills.
By Barbara Gregorich, 48 pages, paperback
ISBN 0-673-18176-6

How to Teach the Letters

This D'Nealian® preschool book is designed for parents who want to help their children learn to recognize letters and their proper construction. It is not designed to teach children to write or pen their letters, although for some it could be used for that purpose.

Audio-oral (hearing-speaking) directions for making each letter are given on each page and should be read to the child as he or she *finger* traces over each letter.

It is imperative that parents understand that not all children learn at the same speed. Children learn best when they are ready! No one, for example, can force a child to walk, talk, or ride a bike, but when a child is ready for such tasks he or she will learn them with ease. Parents should also be aware that girls develop faster than boys during the primary years. Naturally then, girls tend to outperform boys during early growth and development.

Children normally walk after crawling, standing, falling, and stumbling. It happens for most around the age of twelve months. They normally learn to talk after cooing, babbling, and using single words, short phrases, and finally, simple sentences. This usually happens over a twelve to twenty-four month period. Children's ability to learn reading comes after they develop the necessary vision, hearing, and talking skills, along with a longer attention span and abstracting abilities. They are usually ready for formalized reading about age six and a half.

Children normally learn to write after they have scribbled lines and curves, have developed some simple drawing skills, have learned to bridge lines to circles, and have attempted to form or write some letters. They often start by wanting to write their name. Children are usually ready for formal handwriting at about age six. They should not be forced into learning skills before they have developed their readiness.

It is essential to work slowly with the preschoolers. They must have a good perception of how each letter, in each grouping, is made. Without this understanding it is difficult for them to remember the differences among letters.

Children must be aware that *around down* means to "start *counterclockwise* and go around, then down"; that *starting high and slanting down* means to "start higher than middle-size letters." They need to be aware that *under the water* means "*extend* the line down below the baseline," and that a *monkey tail* means to "round up and stop at the end of a letter." Also they must be reminded frequently to start at the dots and follow directional arrows.

Audio directions for making each letter are found on each page and should be read to the child as he or she finger traces over each letter.

It is paramount to synchronize the oral directions with the child's finger tracing. It will be helpful for both the parent and the child to say the directions together as the child finger traces.

After the child is familiar with a letter, he or she may use crayons to trace over the letters or color the pictures.

The words under each picture are not meant to be written or read by the child. They are there only to show that when letters are put together they make words.

Letters are presented in groups of similar design. Alphabetical order is not important at this time. The letters a, d, o, g, c, e, and s are learned first. Except for the letter e, these all start with the same terminology: *around down*. However, after the *curved line up* in forming the letter e, the directions follow the *around down* flow.

The tall letters are taught next. It should be stressed that all tall letters—f, b, l, t, h, and k—are made about twice the height of mid-size letters. The last group of letters comprises i, u, w, y, j, r, n, m, p, q, v, z, and x.

The purpose of this D'Nealian® book is to introduce letters. By using oral directions and finger tracing over the letters, children begin to use their visual (letter recognition), auditory (hearing), and kinesthetic (touch) senses together in the learning process. This method offers the best possible way to entrench information in the memory bank.

Parents should not be concerned that D'Nealian® letters do not look exactly like print letters; this is writing-manuscript print, not typeset book print.

For those children who want to write their letters, unlined paper is acceptable in the beginning. However, when formalized writing starts, the child needs lines to aid in neatness. An example of D'Nealian® writing paper can be found on the inside back cover of *D'Nealian® Handwriting Readiness for Preschoolers, Book 2.*

Parents can best help their children by being patient and positive and by encouraging them when working. Other activities that help readiness for writing are: cutting paper, painting, drawing, hammering, sewing, tying, sculpting with clay, mud, or plasticine, playing with push-pull toys, block building, rolling balls, and playing finger games.

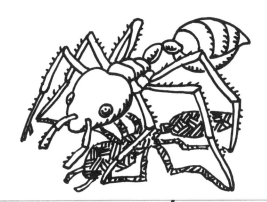

ant

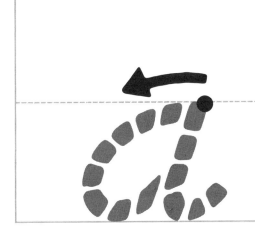

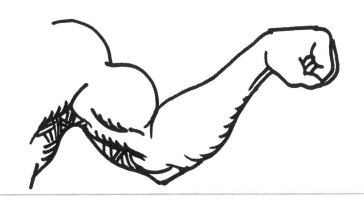

arm

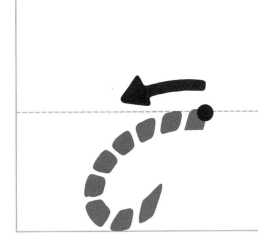

airplane

Middle start; around down, close up, down, and a monkey tail.

From D'Nealian® Handwriting Readiness for Preschoolers, Book 1, Copyright © 1987 Scott, Foresman and Company.

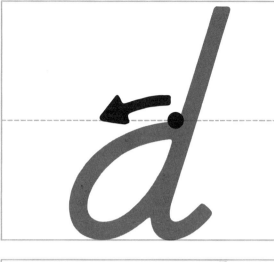

duck

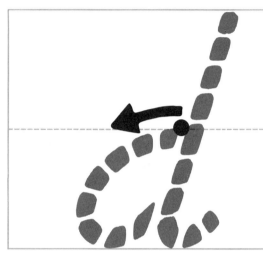
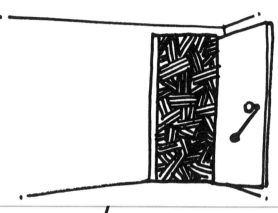

door

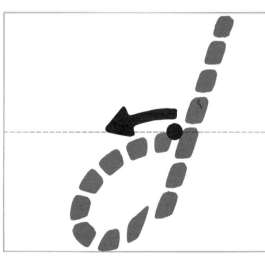

dog

Middle start; around down, touch, up high, down, and a monkey tail.

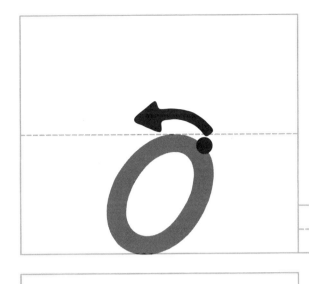

orange

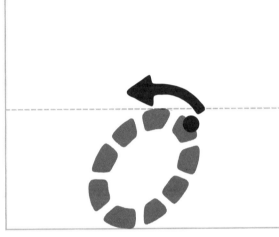

owl

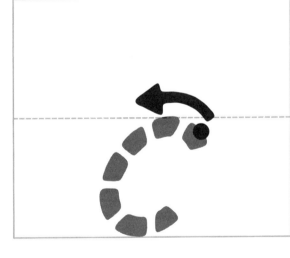

octopus

Middle start; around down, and close up.

From D'Nealian® Handwriting Readiness for Preschoolers, Book 1, Copyright © 1987 Scott, Foresman and Company.

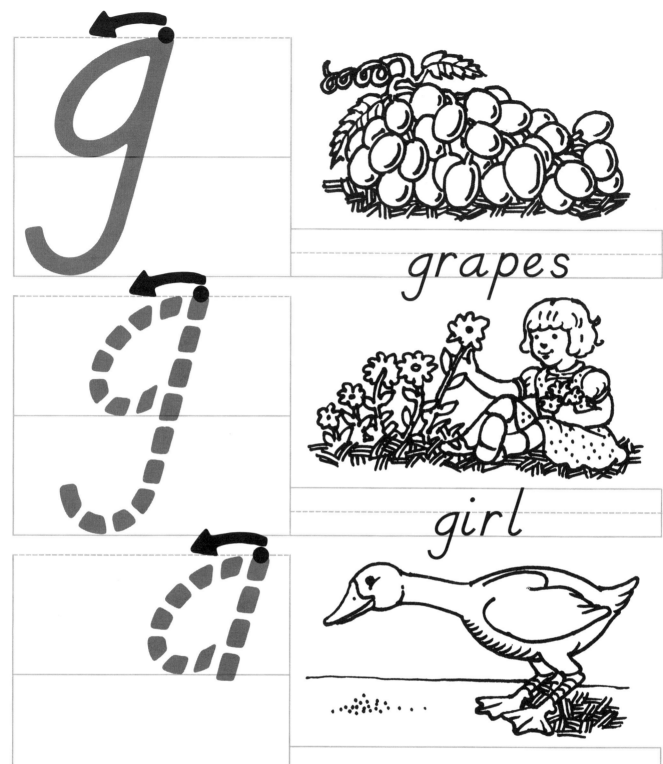

grapes

girl

goose

Middle start; around down,
close up, down under water,
and a fishhook.

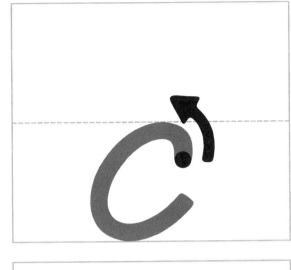

cat

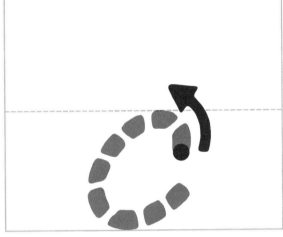

cake

can

Start below the middle;
curve up, around, down, up,
and stop.

From D'Nealian® Handwriting Readiness for Preschoolers, Book 1, Copyright © 1987 Scott, Foresman and Company.

elbow

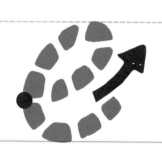

eight

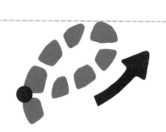

egg

Start between the middle and bottom; curve up, around, touch, down, up, and stop.

From D'Nealian® Handwriting Readiness for Preschoolers, Book 1, Copyright © 1987 Scott, Foresman and Company.

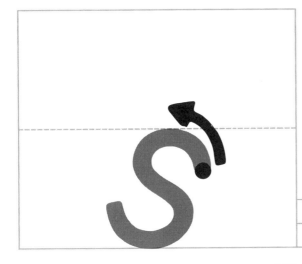

seven

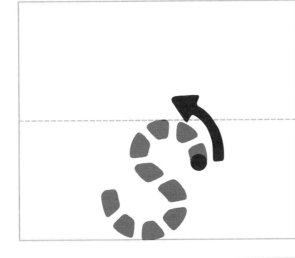

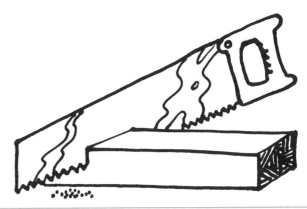

saw

shoe

Start below the middle;
curve up, around, down,
and a snake tail.

From D'Nealian® Handwriting Readiness for Preschoolers, Book 1, Copyright © 1987 Scott, Foresman and Company.

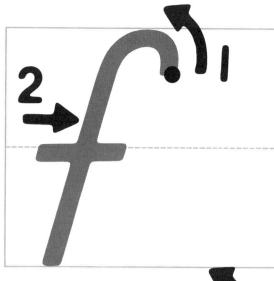

five

face

four

Start below the top; curve
up, around, and slant down.
Cross.

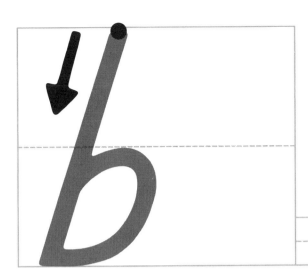

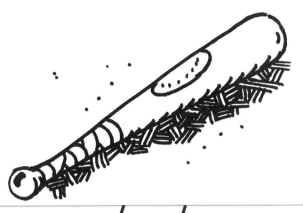

bat

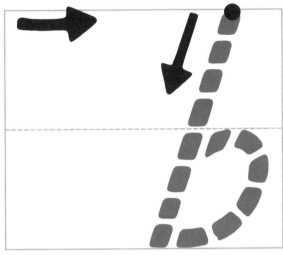

bike

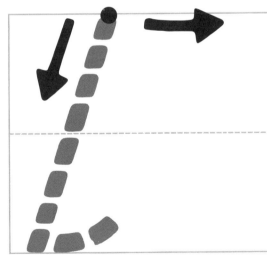

ball

Top start; slant down, around, up, and a tummy.

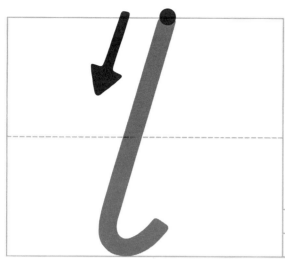

ladder

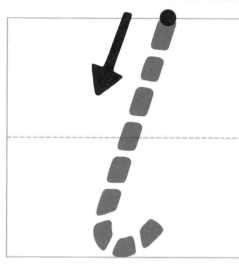

leaf

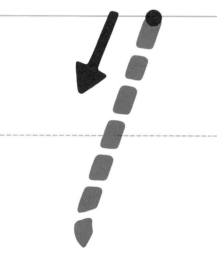

lamp

Top start; slant down,
and a monkey tail.

From *D'Nealian® Handwriting Readiness for Preschoolers, Book 1,* Copyright © 1987 Scott, Foresman and Company.

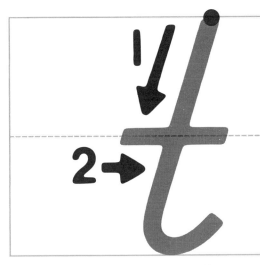

ten

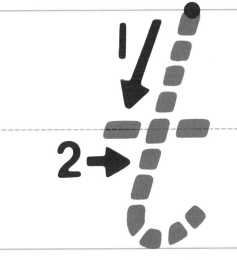

tire

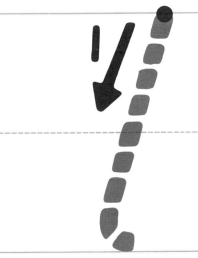

two

*Top start; slant down,
and a monkey tail. Cross.*

From *D'Nealian® Handwriting Readiness for Preschoolers, Book 1,* Copyright © 1987 Scott, Foresman and Company.

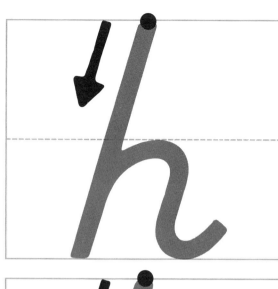

hand

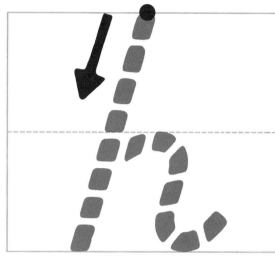

hat

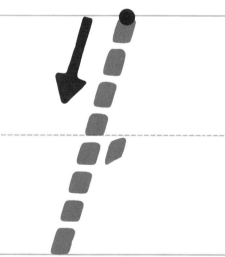

heart

Top start; slant down,
up over the hill, and a
monkey tail.

From D'Nealian® Handwriting Readiness for Preschoolers, Book 1. Copyright © 1987 Scott, Foresman and Company.

kite

kitty

key

Top start; slant down, up into a little tummy; and a monkey tail.

From D'Nealian® Handwriting Readiness for Preschoolers, Book 1, Copyright © 1987 Scott, Foresman and Company.

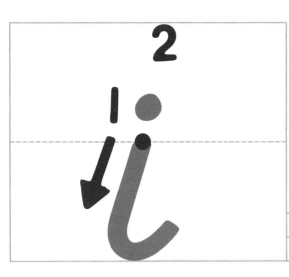

ice cream

iron

igloo

Middle start; slant down,
and a monkey tail.
Add a dot.

From D'Nealian® Handwriting Readiness for Preschoolers, Book 1, Copyright © 1987 Scott, Foresman and Company.

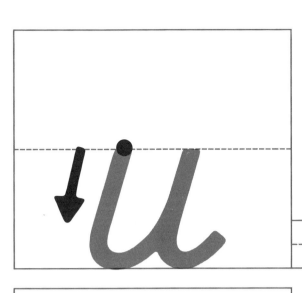

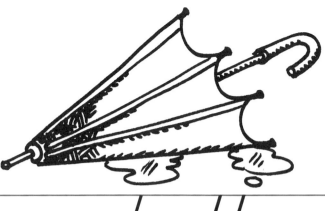

umbrella

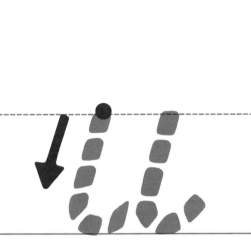

umpire

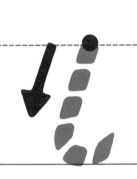

up

Middle start; down, around, up, down, and a monkey tail.

From D'Nealian® Handwriting Readiness for Preschoolers, Book 1, Copyright © 1987 Scott, Foresman and Company.

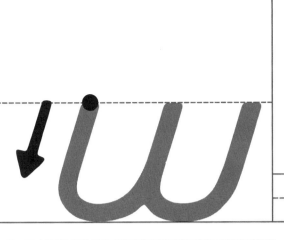

water

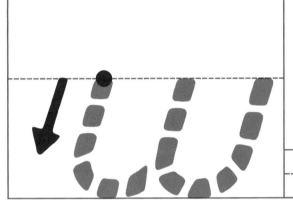

watch

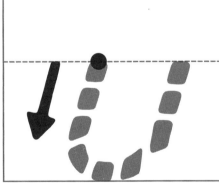

window

Middle start; down,
around, up, and down,
around, up again.

From D'Nealian® Handwriting Readiness for Preschoolers, Book 1, Copyright © 1987 Scott, Foresman and Company.

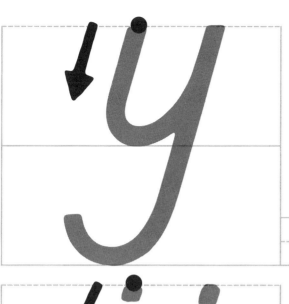

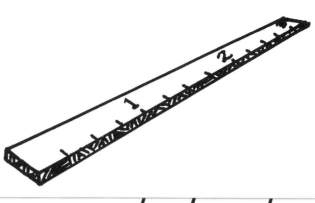

yardstick

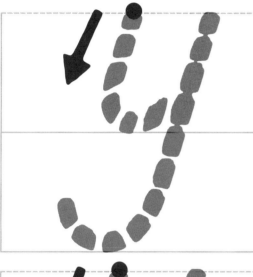

yacht

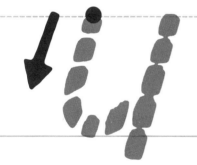

yo-yo

Middle start; down, around,
up, down under water,
and a fishhook.

From D'Nealian® Handwriting Readiness for Preschoolers, Book 1, Copyright © 1987 Scott, Foresman and Company.

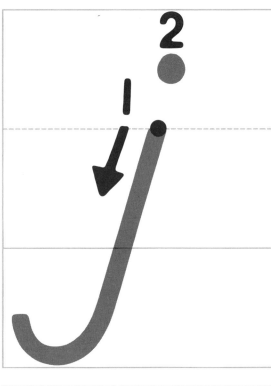

jet

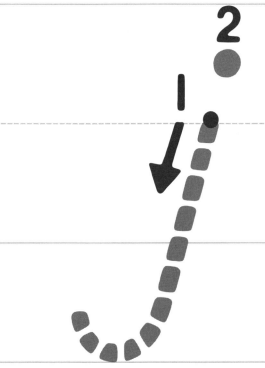

jar

Middle start; slant down under water, and a fishhook. Add a dot.

From D'Nealian® Handwriting Readiness for Preschoolers, Book 1. Copyright © 1987 Scott, Foresman and Company.

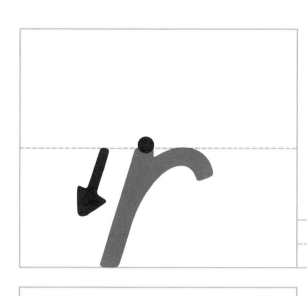

rabbit

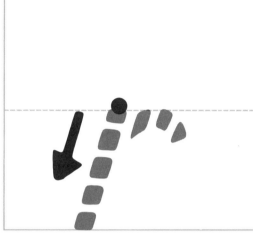

ribbon

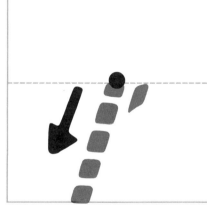

ring

Middle start; slant down, up, and a roof.

From D'Nealian® Handwriting Readiness for Preschoolers, Book 1, Copyright © 1987 Scott, Foresman and Company.

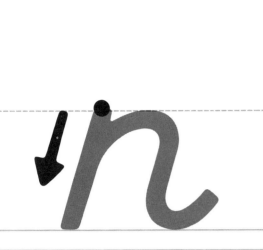

nose

nine

nest

Middle start; slant down,
up over the hill, and
a monkey tail.

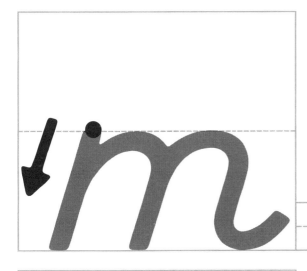

mouse

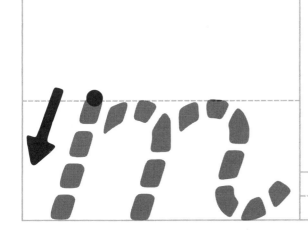

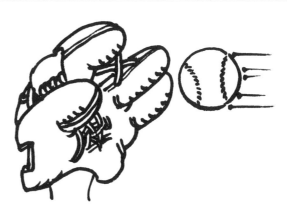

mitt

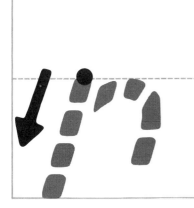

monkey

Middle start; slant down, up
over the hill, up over the hill
again, and a monkey tail.

From D'Nealian® Handwriting Readiness for Preschoolers, Book 1, Copyright © 1987 Scott, Foresman and Company.

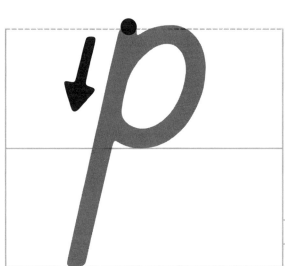

pear

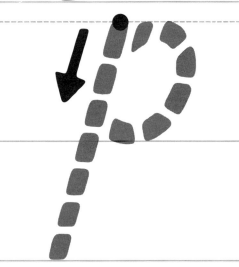

pig

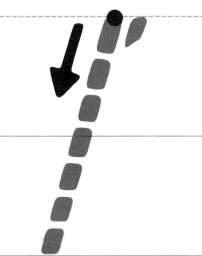

pie

Middle start; slant down
under water, up, around,
and a tummy.

From D'Nealian® Handwriting Readiness for Preschoolers, Book 1, Copyright © 1987 Scott, Foresman and Company.

quarter

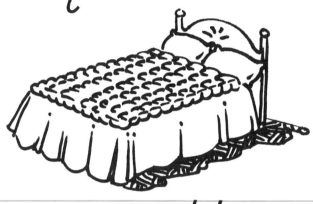

quilt

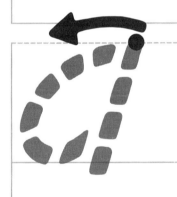

queen

Middle start; around down,
close up, down under water,
and a backwards fishhook.

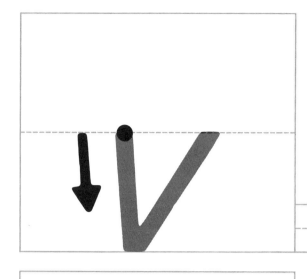

vase

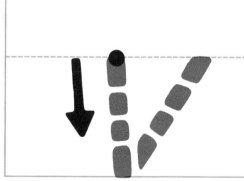

violin

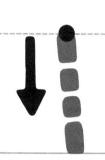

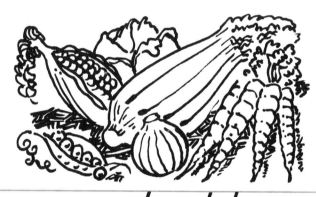

vegetables

Middle start; slant down
right, and slant up right.

zero

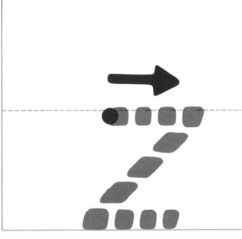

zebra

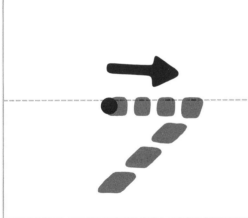

zipper

*Middle start; over right,
slant down left, and
over right.*

From D'Nealian® Handwriting Readiness for Preschoolers, Book 1, Copyright © 1987 Scott, Foresman and Company.

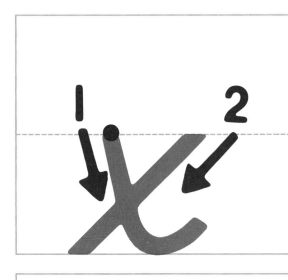

ox

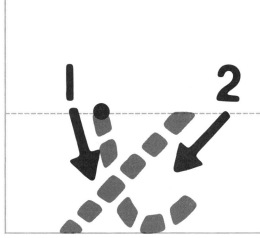

ax

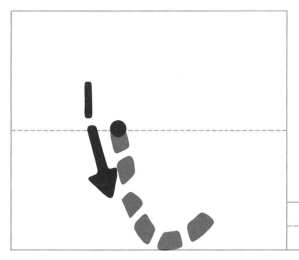

fox

Middle start; slant down
right, and a monkey tail.
Cross down left.

From D'Nealian® Handwriting Readiness for Preschoolers, Book 1, Copyright © 1987 Scott, Foresman and Company.

1 ☆

2 ☆ ☆

3 ☆ ☆ ☆

4 ☆ ☆ ☆ ☆

5 ☆ ☆
☆ ☆

6 ☆ ☆ ☆
☆ ☆

7 ☆ ☆ ☆ ☆
☆ ☆

8 ☆ ☆ ☆ ☆ ☆
☆ ☆

9 ☆ ☆ ☆ ☆ ☆ ☆
☆ ☆

10 ☆ ☆ ☆ ☆
☆ ☆ ☆ ☆ ☆

A B C D E

F G H I J K

L M N O P

Q R S T U

V W X Y Z

28